ECOSYSTEM FACTS THAT YOU SHOULD KNOW

THE FORESTS EDITION

Nature Picture Books | Children's Nature Books

Speedy Publishing LLC
40 E. Main St. #1156
Newark, DE 19711
www.speedypublishing.com

Forests come in many types, from rain forests in the topics to stands of giant redwood trees in northwestern North America. Walk into the forest and learn about this wonderful part of our world!

Earth trail through idyllic Sequoia grove
Redwood National Park forest California

INTO THE FOREST

A forest is a part of the world where the dominant growing things are trees and other plants with woody stems. But there is a lot more in a forest than just trees!.

All sorts of animals live in forests, from the birds and squirrels that make their nests in the trees to the animals that burrow in among the roots. There is a whole world of insects and microbes on the leaves and bark of the trees, and down in the forest floor. Both plant-eating and meat-eating animals can live in the forest, and humans use what the forest grows for everything from building supplies to medicines.

Deer in the forest.

Mountain landscape and sunrise

THE FIVE-LAYER FOREST

Most forests have different things going on at different layers, and only the trees themselves may touch all five layers of the forest.

THE FOREST FLOOR

Without rich soil making up the forest floor, the trees would not survive and there would be no forest. Falling leaves, decaying fallen trees, animal waste, and materials from smaller plants make up the forest floor.

Tree roots dig down into the forest floor for two reasons: to find and deliver the nutrients the tree needs to survive, and to provide strong support so high winds won't easily knock the tree over.

All sorts of insects and animal life make their home in the forest floor, from butterflies and spiders to worms and even some birds. There are also billions of microbes, which you can only see with a microscope, busily processing the soil.

Spider in amazon rainforest, Brazil.

Not all forest floors work the same. In the rain forest, the soil is very poor in some minerals and nutrients, and the forests only survive because the whole process of decay of plant matter and recycling of its nutrients is very fast.

Snowdrop flowers growing on forest floor.

THE HERBACEOUS LAYER

The next layer starts at the top of the forest floor and extends up a few feet. It includes seedlings of young trees, other bushes and small plants, ferns and flowers, and mosses that grow on rocks and on the trunks of the trees. Aside from the seedlings, these plants don't ever grow very tall. They are designed to live in the shade and moisture under the trees.

Biogradska Gora National Park, Montenegro.

THE SHRUB LAYER

The shrub layer overlaps the herbaceous layer. It includes young trees and shrubs, which are plants with several woody stems. Shrubs can grow to between ten and twenty feet tall, but they still are under the shadow of the trees. Many types of birds, insects, lizards, and spiders make their homes in the shrub layer.

Redwood National Park

THE UNDERSTORY

The understory has the growing and leafy tops of younger trees, and the still-active branches of the tallest trees that are not right at the top. The layer above protects the understory from extremes of weather, but lets less light through, so trees at this level grow more slowly.

Many animals live in the understory: birds of all sorts, of course; and frogs and mammals like raccoons and squirrels. Butterflies and caterpillars fill this layer in temperate zones; in the tropics this is the home for many types of monkeys.

A forest of tree canopies.

THE CANOPY

The tops of the tallest, oldest trees in the forest make up the canopy. This area can be 200 feet above the forest floor. The canopy gets most of the sunlight available, but also has to deal with strong winds, harsh rain and sleet, and even lightning strikes.

The residents of the canopy include birds, snakes, tree frogs, lizards, and insects with sturdy bodies.

Some redwood trees are so big, and grow so tall, that in their canopies they are hosts to whole miniature forests!

Temperate rainforest.

FOREST TREES COOPERATE

Trees don't just stand around! Not only are they busy making energy by combining sunlight and water in the process called photosynthesis, they are also sharing with and supporting nearby trees of the same species.

The roots of trees of the same species touch each other underground, and they can pass nutrients and other materials to the tree most in need of them. Even what looks like the stump of a dead tree can still, under the ground, be a living contributor to the nutrient transfer to its cousins.

When insects attack a tree, the tree can send out a chemical signal that blows downwind to warn other trees about the problem. The other trees can even change their taste so the insects won't want to eat them!

When high winds blow, trees that are in danger of toppling over lean against their neighbors for support. When the storm is over, the tree slowly regains its balance.

Scarab beetle on a tree.

Forest floor.

FUN FOREST FACTS

RAIN FOREST DIVERSITY

More animal and plant species live in the rain forest than in any other habitat on dry land on Earth. The rain forest in Indonesia has more than 20% of all types of plant and animal life.

RAIN FORESTS DON'T HAVE TO BE TROPICAL

In the west of Canada is the Great Bear rain forest, primarily made up of Sitka spruce. People who make musical instruments like violins and guitars prefer to work with wood from these trees.

Wild Mushroom.

PHARMACY FORESTS

More than a quarter of the medicine we use comes from substances found in plants that grow in rain forests. And there are far more plants that we have not studied to see how they might help us.

THE WORLD'S LUNGS

Forests help keep the world's climate stable by converting carbon dioxide, CO_2, into oxygen, and providing a cooling effect for the ground under the shade of the forest canopy.

THE BIGGEST TREE-DWELLERS

Orangutans are primates that spend most of their time in trees. They build nests for sleeping, and use sticks to get honey out of bees' nests and grubs out of logs.

TALLEST TREE

The tallest tree that we know of that is still living is a coast redwood in California which is over 350 feet tall. The largest tree by volume is a giant sequoia in the same area of North America. Its trunk measures more than 30 feet around.

Grove of Giant Sequoias, Sequoia National Park.

THE OLDEST LIVING TREE?

There are two types of trees: those that grow from seeds and those that grow from the roots of the parent tree. The trees that grow from seeds or from the original roots are called non-clonal. The oldest non-clonal tree we have found so far is a Great Basin bristlecone pine in California's White Mountains.

It is probably more than five thousand years old. Another non-clonal tree, but one where a new trunk grew from the original roots after the first trunk died, is almost ten thousand years old.

THE TREMBLING GIANT

Clonal trees are like a colony of trees all related to the central parent. The first tree puts out a strong network of roots, and then child trees grow up out of the ground from those roots, forming a circle or a grove around the parent. The oldest clonal tree community we know of is a colony of quaking aspen trees called "Pando". A single, complex root system supports the whole colony of trees, and Pando is probably more than 80,000 years old!

Quaking Aspens.

A FOREST SAVES AN ISLAND

In India, a man named Jadav Payeng was worried about erosion destroying Majuli Island. He planted a forest bigger than New York City's Central Park to stabilize the island and save it from destruction. The forest is now home to a wide range of wildlife and insects, and other species of plants, and the island is not washing away.

Tropical forest

GOOD BREATHING

When you walk in a pine forest the air not only smells good, it does good things for your breathing. The trees generate a compound called a-Pinene, which doctors use to help people with asthma and other breathing problems. When you walk among the pine trees, you get a-Pinene without a prescription!

Young woman enjoying the fresh air.

A GOOD SIDE EFFECT OF A BAD THING

Genghis Kahn was the leader of the Mongol people as they conquered much of Asia. They destroyed many other nations, and killed as many as 40 million people. With that many people dead, a lot of farmland became fallow and over time turned back into forest land. The effect was large enough to cool the Earth's climate significantly.

Young couple walking through the forest.

GOING, GONE

Over 80% of the Earth's natural forests have been destroyed.

GREAT GREEN BELTS

In China and Africa, governments have started programs to fight the growth of deserts. They are planting wide belts of new forests to defend the land from the desert sands.

Trees being planted.

Hiker walking through the forest.

TAKE A WALK IN THE WOODS

Forests are essential to life on Earth. They help the planet thrive and keep in balance. Read other Baby Professor books, like ***What Every Child should Know about Climate Change***, to learn why this is important.

Is there a forest near you? Go for a walk among the trees and think about how different their life is from yours, but also about how you are connected in life together on this one Earth.

www.ingramcontent.com/pod-product-compliance
Lightning Source LLC
LaVergne TN
LVHW080047170826
845677LV00024B/1630

* 9 7 9 8 8 6 9 4 3 8 6 5 2 *